The Canary Cage
A drama
Diana Raffle

New Theatre Publications - London
www.plays4theatre.com

© 2013 BY Diana Raffle
First published in 2004

The edition published in 2013

New Theatre Publications

2 Hereford Close | Warrington | Cheshire | WA1 4HR | 01925 485605

www.plays4theatre.com   email: info@plays4theatre.com

New Theatre Publications is the trading name of the publishing house that is owned by members of the Playwrights' Co-operative. This innovative project was launched on the 1st October 1997 by writers Paul Beard and Ian Hornby with the aim of encouraging the writing and promotion of the very best in New Theatre by Professional and Amateur writers for the Professional and Amateur Theatre at home and abroad.

ISBN 9 781 840 94929 2

Characters

Debra Chambers
Jean Hammond
Mary Perkins
Dave Porter

4

Copyright Information

The play is fully protected under the Copyright laws of the British Commonwealth of Nations, the United States of America and all countries of the Berne and Universal Copyright Conventions.

All rights including Stage, Motion Picture, Radio, television, Public Reading, and Translation into Foreign Languages, are strictly reserved.

No part of this publication may lawfully be reproduced in ANY form or by any means - photocopying, typescript, recording (including video-recording), manuscript, electronic, mechanical or otherwise - or be transmitted or stored in a retrieval system, without prior permission.

Licenses for amateur performances are issued subject to the understanding that it shall be made clear in all advertising matter that the audience will witness an amateur performance; that the names of the authors of the plays shall be included on all programmes, and that the integrity of the authors' work will be preserved.

The Royalty Fee is subject to contract and subject to variation at the sole discretion of New Theatre Publications.

In Theatres of Halls seating Four Hundred or more the fee will be subject to negotiation.

In Territories Overseas the fee quoted may not apply. A fee will be quoted on application to New Theatre Publications, London.

Video-Recording of Amateur Productions

Please note that the copyright laws governing video-recording are extremely complex and that it should not be assumed that any play may be video-recorded for whatever purpose without first obtaining the permission of the appropriate agents. The fact that a play is published by New Theatre Publications does not indicate that video rights are available or that New Theatre Publications control such rights.

Performing Licence Applications

A performing licence for these plays will be issued by "New Theatre Publications" subject to the following conditions.

Conditions

1.   That the performance fee is paid in full on the date of application for a licence.

2.   That the name of the author(s) is/are clearly shown in any programme or publicity material.

3.   That the author(s) is/are entitled to receive two complimentary tickets to see his/her/their work in performance if they so wish.

4.   That a copy of the play is purchased from New Theatre Publications for each named speaking part and a minimum of three copies purchased for backstage use.

5.   That a copy of any review be forwarded to New Theatre Publications.

6.   That the New Theatre Publications logo is clearly shown on any publicity material. This is available on our website.

Fees

Details of script prices and fees payable for each performance or public reading can be obtained by telephone to (+44) 01925 485605 or to the address below.

Alternatively, latest prices can be obtained from our website www.plays4theatre.com where credit/debit cards can be used for payment.

To apply for a performing licence for any play please write to New Theatre Publications 2 Hereford Close, Warrington, Cheshire WA1 4HR or email info@plays4theatre.com with the following details:-

1.   Name and address of theatre company.

2.   Details of venue including seating capacity.

3.   Dates of proposed performance or public reading.

4.   Contact telephone number for Author's complimentary tickets.

Or apply directly via our website at www.plays4theatre.com

The Canary Cage
by Diana Raffle
Characters
Debra Chambers
Jean Hammond
Mary Perkins
Dave Porter

A cellar, so the stage should be set with junk, old boxes etc. Set of steps SL. Curtains open onto a dark stage with a spotlight shining on Mary who is kneeling C wearing a long nightdress. Mary is repeatedly reciting the Lord's Prayer, her hands clasped together, completely unaware of anything around her. Suddenly a shaft of light/torch light appears at the top of the steps, finally resting on Mary.

Debra *(from top of steps)* Mrs Hammond, I've found her, she's down here.

Jean *(off)* Is she all right?

Debra *(coming down steps)* I can't see. Do you know where the light switch is?

Jean *(from top of the stairs)* Try over by the cold water tank, that's where mine is… no, to your left.

Debra Got it.

(Lights up, Debra rushes towards Mary who does not react to their entry but continues to kneel and recite the prayer. Jean comes down steps.)

Debra Auntie Mary, are you all right? We've been looking everywhere for you. *(Jean moves further D towards Debra.)*

Jean Hello Mary dear.

Debra Mrs Hammond helped me look, didn't you.

Jean Yes, we've both been trying to find you. We've been worried about you.

Debra I don't think she can hear us.

Jean Perhaps she doesn't want to hear us.

Debra Auntie, why don't we get you upstairs in the warm, it's too damp down here, you could get a chill or something.

Jean I'll make us a nice cup of tea and then you can tell us what's on your mind.

(Debra tries to put her jacket around Mary's shoulders. Mary

reacts and Debra pulls back leaving Mary to rock backwards and forwards.)

Debra Aunt Mary what's the matter? Why is she doing that? She looks like one of Dad's day care patients.

Jean I don't think your aunt is very well at the moment Debra.

Debra I can see that, perhaps we ought to call someone.

Jean I'll do it, your aunt's with the same doctor as me, I've got his number in my bag.

Debra Auntie, do you think you could make it upstairs?

(Debra takes hold of Mary's arm. Mary appears distressed and begins to rock more violently.)

Jean I should leave her be dear I don't think we should try and move her, the doctor will sort her out. Look you stay with her while I go and make the phone call.

Debra Don't be long. *(Jean exits. Debra sits quietly for a moment. Mary is still repeating the prayer but very quietly now, under her breath.)* It's OK Auntie, Mrs Hammond has gone in to alert the task force, so any minute now we should get the SAS lowering themselves down the drainpipes. *(Debra looks towards her for a reaction, none is forthcoming.)* It's awfully dark and dingy down here Auntie. What made you come down? Has something happened?

Jean *(off)* It's engaged at the moment, I've put the kettle on so I'll keep trying while I'm waiting.

Debra OK.

Jean Does your aunt take sugar?

Debra Yes..I mean I think so. I'm not really sure.

Jean I'll just bring down the bowl then, she can put it in herself. You just keep talking, I'm sure that will help.

Debra *(looks around)* Talking… right.

Debra It must be handy having a cellar, somewhere to keep all your junk. We have to keep ours in the garage. Tom says it's these modern houses, they don't build them with any storage space he says. Did I tell you that Tom had been promoted. Yes, he's head chef at the Lemon Tree now. It's a real promotion this time, he says. I don't get to see much of him though, his hours are a bit hectic and they need him to be there a lot more now, but the money's better. I thought I might get a few tidbits back from the menu but no chance. Tom says it's health and safety rules or something, no doggy bags allowed.. So I can't tell you if the foods good, but he smells nice when I see him. Here, we should go there shouldn't we, when you're better. We should book a table and surprise him. Hey, we could even send the meal back, make a complaint about the rotten cook or something, imagine Tom's face eh… he'd kill me! *(Pauses and looks a little uncomfortable.)* I know you never liked Tom much, but he's a good man really, he's just a bit weak. Like this thing with Melanie, I know it'll all blow over after a couple of weeks, like the thing with Dawn… Anyway I'm letting him have some space for a while, well, Tom thought it would be a good idea, so, he's moved out. So he can think more clearly he says, and to be honest it's not so bad having the place to myself. At least I can watch what I like on the Tele, that sort of thing. And I'm sure he'll be back soon, he has to come back doesn't he… doesn't he?

Jean *(enters with a small tea tray. The tray holds three cups and saucers, a bowl of sugar lumps and a small fruit knife)* Everything OK ladies? Here I am with a good old fashioned cup of tea, guaranteed to revive us all. I could only find sugar lumps so I brought a little knife too, in case your aunt only liked half a spoonful.

Debra Oh thanks Mrs Hammond. Did you manage to get through to the doctor?

Jean No, I'm afraid it was still engaged. I'll pop up again in a minute. How's everything down here?

Debra No change I'm afraid.

Jean Well let's have this cup before it goes cold. It was blowing a gale out there when I was making the tea and your aunt has left one of the kitchen windows open. I wonder if you wouldn't mind closing it for her, my hands aren't so good with those catches..

(There is a loud bang as the cellar door bangs shut.)

Debra Wasn't that the door?

Jean It must have been the wind.

Debra *(gets up and goes to the door, already a little panicky)* It will still open though won't it. I mean its not locked now or anything is it?

Jean I hope not, mine has a handle on both sides of the door.

Debra Well this one hasn't. Oh my god, we're locked in.

Jean Now don't panic dear. I'm sure we're not locked in.

Debra Well what would you call it then… temporarily unable to escape?

Jean *(gets up and tries the door)* Here let me try.

Debra What are we going to do? Nobody even knows we're down here.

Jean Well you do appear to be right… it's impossible to open it from inside.

Debra Oh my god. *(Debra bangs on door.)* Help. hellllllp..can anybody hear me… we're locked in… helllllp.

Jean *(comes back.)* Now calm down dear, there must be a way out

Debra Where?

Jean Well I don't know, but there's no need to panic just yet

Debra Really? So when do you suggest that I panic then, next week when I've starved to death?

Jean Oh don't be so melodramatic, it won't come to that, and besides it'll take more than a week to starve to death. Look at that magician fellow, he managed to stay alive just by drinking water for forty days.

Debra Yes but we don't have any water do we… just three cups of tea and a bowl of sugar.

Jean Look, sooner or later somebody is going to notice that we are missing and put two and two together and find us.

Debra Oh right, so who is going to come looking for you… your husband.? Oh no, don't think so.. you don't have a husband do you? Or a partner or a vaguely interested third party, because unless you have forgotten Mrs Hammond, you live alone, so that leaves us completely up the swanny, unless your cat has learnt to dial 999.

Jean So? What about you. You have a husband don't you? Tim or whatever his name is.

Debra His name is Tom

Jean Well there you are then. I'm sure that Tom will be anxiously searching for you as soon as you don't appear home for tea.

(As they talk, Mary looks around her and sees the small knife on the tray, she reaches out and takes it, slipping it into her pocket.)

Debra He's not at home.

Jean Well when he gets back then

Debra He's not coming back.

Jean You mean he's left you?

Debra No, course not

Jean Well where is he then? Has he gone away on a trip or something?

Debra   No… not that. It's just… look it doesn't matter why, it's none of your business, what matters is that we are locked in Auntie Mary's cellar.

Jean   But then that means that nobody knows we are here.

Debra   Oh at last the penny's dropped.

Jean   Look there's no need to be rude. It's not my fault we're down here. I was only trying to help you if you remember, you were the one worried about your aunt, not me.

Debra   Yes, yes, I know. I'm sorry, it's just I'm scared. I mean, we could be down here forever..three rat gnawed skeletons propped up against the walls.

Jean   Now, now really, I'm sure that it won't come to that. Sooner or later somebody's going to come looking for us. Look, I tell you what why don't we have our tea whilst it's still warm and try to calm down a little. I'm a great believer in keeping calm in a crisis you know .

Debra   Shouldn't we conserve our fluids, after all it could be a while before we are found.

Jean   Well I hardly think it's necessary but you do whatever makes you feel better. Personally I'm not going to let a good cup of tea go cold on the off chance, all we need is for one of the other neighbors to come knocking and we could be out in half an hour. *(Picks up her cup.)*

Debra   Perhaps you're right. I'll have a few sips at least and save the rest for later just in case. *(Picks up her cup and takes a small sip.)*

Jean   This floor is filthy.

Debra   *(puts down her cup and begins searching through the junk.)* I suppose we ought to find something more comfortable to sit on if we are going to be here for a while.

Jean   Isn't that an old deck chair over there?

Debra   What this, oh yes..so it is..Here, you can have it if you can put it up. *(Passes it to Jean.)* I'm hopeless with those things. Aha. *(Debra finds an old cushion and putting it down sits down.)* This will do nicely.

   (Jean sits on deck chair.)

Debra   Do you think she can hear us?

Jean   Well if she can, she doesn't seem particularly interested.

Debra   I wonder what happened, what made her come down here, it's so depressing. It's as though she wants to shut herself away from the world.

Jean   And now we are all in the same boat.

Debra   Only we didn't choose to be.

Jean   Perhaps your aunt didn't choose this either, perhaps whatever it is that's upset her so much has caused her mind to withdraw her from life for a while, to protect her.

Debra   But what could have upset her? She taught English by correspondence, she was hardly living a life of intrigue.

Jean   How would you know? You didn't exactly spend a lot of time with her.

Debra   So, it's not because I didn't care. I just had a lot on, what with work and Tom and everything and besides even if I had come to see my aunt more often it doesn't mean to say I could have prevented anything from happening.

Jean   Perhaps she wouldn't have come to this.

Debra   Oh thanks for those few words of comfort.

Jean   Well, what do you want me to say? Things that would make you feel better? Call me a nosy old wotsit if you like but I never saw so much as a soul visit your aunt in the past few months. The closest she ever got to a conversation was a quick chat with the milkman on a Saturday morning.

Debra   The milkman! Oh thank god for the milkman. Why didn't I think of that. He's bound to come looking if Auntie doesn't open the door. Well, at least I can sit here knowing we aren't going to shrivel up and die anymore.

Jean   Nice to know you were listening to something I said at least.

Debra   I was listening… to all of it. I just think that you are being unfair that's all

Jean   I suppose you were just living a busy life, isn't that what people say.

Debra   I am busy as it happens, very busy. Although to be honest Mrs Hammond, I really don't think that my relationship with my aunt is any of your business and I would appreciate it if we could talk about something else whilst we are down here.

Jean   *(takes a long sip of tea)* Suit yourself dear.

             (Lights down to denote passing of time. Lights up, Mary is no longer C, but UC. Jean and Debra asleep, Mary moans softly, waking Debra)

Debra *(looking around)* Auntie... is that you..? *(Jean wakes.)* Mrs Hammond, she's gone.

Jean Mmm? Oh dear yes. Mary? Mary dear, where are you?

Debra *(sees her Mary and goes to her. Mary is gently rocking and mumbling softly to herself)* Auntie, Auntie it's me... Debra, are you OK?

Jean She must have moved whilst we were asleep

Debra Auntie, you must be freezing, here let me... *(Tries to put an old blanket around her shoulders, Mary becomes agitated and Debra backs off.)*

Jean Come away for a minute, leave her be, perhaps she'll feel more at ease.

Debra I hate seeing her like this.

Jean So do I dear, but nowadays there are doctors specially for this kind of thing and who's to say that with a few drugs and some therapy she might be right as rain before you know it. *(Debra looks upset.)* And it's not too cold down here, I'm sure she'll survive until we get out.

Debra If we ever get out, you mean. How long were we asleep?

Jean *(looks at her watch)* About four hours.

Debra It seems like days.

Jean That's because you have a life up there, for people like me this is just life without the television.

Debra Don't you get out much then either?

Jean No, not much.. You would have thought living so close to your aunt we would have been good company for each other wouldn't you? But we weren't, she lived behind her curtain and I lived behind mine

Debra Why?

Jean Why? Why didn't we speak? What was there to say. I had my demons, and she had hers.

Debra I don't see what you mean.

Jean No, I don't suppose that you do dear, our eyes have a horrible habit of deceiving us don't you think, we think we see things clearly and yet we don't, we really don't you know.

Debra You're not making a lot of sense Mrs Hammond

Jean Forgive me, perhaps I should just explain, but first please tell me something. *(Jean stands.)* When you look at me, what do you see? I mean honestly see.

Debra I see a middle aged lady who lives on her own and looks neat and

Jean Harmless?

Debra Well I was going to say tidy but yes, you look harmless. Why, aren't you?

Jean Before I moved into this street, your aunt and I were friends did you know that? *(Debra frowns and shakes her head.)* We lived in the same village

Debra Langley?

Jean Yes, Langley. We grew up there together.

Debra But why didn't my aunt mention anything. Didn't she recognize you?

Jean Oh she recognized me all right, that's why she didn't want anything to do with me.

Debra Why? What had happened between you, did you steal her boyfriend or something?

Jean No... I killed him

Debra You what?

Jean I killed him

Debra You are joking right..?

Jean I only wish I were dear.

Debra Oh this is rubbish, my aunt would have said something.

Jean So she never mentioned Charlie to you?

Debra No, never heard her mention anybody called Charlie to me or anyone else.

Jean Funny, there was a time when she couldn't stop talking about him.

Debra Mrs Hammond, I don't know whether you think this is a game or something but I don't happen to find it particularly amusing. I don't believe for one second that you killed anyone. I think you are just trying to frighten me

Jean And are you frightened?

Debra No, of course not

Jean Good, because I never wanted to scare you dear, I was just trying to explain about me and Mar...

(Mary begins to whimper and rock more violently. Debra rushes

to her and puts her arm around her.)

Debra   There, you see what you've done. You've upset her.

Jean   It's because I mentioned Charlie.

Debra   Oh don't be so ridiculous.

Jean   *(gets up and goes over to Mary)* She can hear us.

Debra   So, that's good isn't it?

Jean   Did you hear me Mary? You remember Charlie don't you. Your sweetheart, the man you were going to marry.

Debra   What do you think you're doing?

(Mary is suddenly still.)

Jean   You thought he loved you didn't you dear? You believed everything he told you, but he was a liar wasn't he Mary… a dirty rotten stinking *liar!*

Mary   *(clasps her hands over her ears and starts to shake her head, then screams)* No… No. No. Noooo…

(Mary collapses into Debra's arms. Lights down. Lights up, Debra is sitting with Mary's head in her lap, she is stroking her hair. Jean is back in the deckchair.)

Jean   *(looking at her watch)* It's nearly midnight. *(Debra ignores her.)* I said, it's nearly midnight.

Debra   *(extricates herself from Mary and comes down)* Why did you do that?

Jean   Because perhaps I'm tired of living behind a curtain

Debra   Oh, so you are going to make everyone else miserable just because you feel like it?

Jean   Well at least it proves that she can hear us.

Debra   Why did you say all that stuff? Couldn't you see how much it was upsetting her?

Jean   Haven't you asked yourself why it upset her so much.

Debra   No, why should I.

Jean   Because it's true, all of it. *(Debra looks angry and moves further down.)* When I asked you to describe me you took it for granted that my name was Hammond didn't you.

Debra   That's because it is.

Jean   No it isn't, that was a name the police gave me when I was released from prison. They wanted to give me a chance to live out my life without reprisals, so I got a new name and a new home. It was the worst kind of irony to see your aunt move in to number 25. However thorough the police had been with me, they never thought to check the movements of your aunt, coincidence is a curious thing, don't you think?

Debra You were in prison?

Jean Oh yes… for twenty four years of my life.

Debra Small price to pay for taking someone's else's life I suppose.

Jean You think I got off lightly?

Debra I don't really think anything at all… No, that's not true, actually, I think you are as screwed up as she is at the moment and quite frankly being locked in a cellar with the pair of you is not exactly how I was planning to spend the night. *(Moves back to cushion and sits.)*

Jean *(moves towards Debra)* My name was Jenny Franklyn, I was sentenced in July 1980. I spent the first fourteen years in Holloway and the last ten in Cookham Wood. I had one daughter, she was given to Charlie's family to raise and I never saw her again.

Debra No..I'm sorry, I still don't believe this.

Jean *(reaches into her pocket and pulls out an old newspaper clipping and passes it to Debra)* I've carried that around since the trial, I don't know why, it's just something to look at when things don't seem real. A reminder that when I wake up in the morning, it wasn't just a nightmare.

Debra Oh my god

Jean *(takes clipping back)* It was a long time ago.

Debra Why did you stay here? If you knew that my aunt had moved so close to you, why didn't you just move on yourself?

Jean I had no money, no job after prison. You have to understand, I wasn't used to being in the outside world.

Debra You could have told the police, got them to move you on

Jean I was frightened, I didn't want to move on.

Debra So you thought that you'd hang around and upset my aunt some more did you? Don't you think you had done enough?

Jean You think I should have let her have some peace?

Debra Why not? She'd done you no harm, it was you. You had obviously destroyed her when you murdered the man she loved. Well, now it all makes sense, why she's like this. It's because she recognized you wasn't it? This is what made her 'withdraw' as you put it..because she didn't want to face any more pain, the pain that you now constantly reminded her of.

Jean Its not as simple as that.

Debra Isn't it? You just couldn't let it go could you. You couldn't do the decent thing and leave her with her memories, you had to stick around taunting her with your freedom and your life, reminding her every day of the life that you took away from Charlie..

Jean You don't understand…,

(Jean and Debra are now standing, facing each other and shouting.)

Debra What… what don't I understand?

Jean It wasn't like that, Mary was…

Debra Mary was what… suffering? Tortured? Knowing that you were so close to her again. You're sick, you know that and when we get out of here I am going to make sure that my aunt is safe and as far away from you as possible.

Jean *(sinks to the floor.)* You don't understand

Debra Just leave me alone.

(Lights down to denote passing of time. Lights up, Debra asleep on the cushion, Jean asleep in deck chair. Mary has moved D and is gently trying to wake Debra.)

Mary Debra.

Debra Auntie? Are you OK?

Mary A little better love. Sorry about that, I suppose I must have frightened you.

Debra I thought you were ill.

Mary Well perhaps I was… a little..it all got a bit too much you see. I just wanted it all to go away.

Debra Oh it's all right I understand everything. I know about Jenny… she told me.

Mary She's a wicked woman Debra.

Debra You don't have to convince me Auntie, to be honest I think she's mad as a hatter.

Mary She wanted him for herself you see, she couldn't bear it that Charlie wanted me instead.

Debra It must have been terrible.

Mary A crime of passion they called it. Everybody knew he had wanted a divorce and yet she wouldn't let him go.

Debra A divorce?

Mary We hadn't meant to fall in love. We didn't plan it or anything, it was just fate..we were meant to be together.

Debra *(confused)* You mean Charlie was Jenny's husband?

Mary What, she didn't tell you that?

Debra No.

Mary I couldn't believe it when I saw her go past my window, I recognized her immediately, believe it or not she hasn't changed that much, prison's obviously been kind to her.

Debra Auntie, you do know that we are locked in down here don't you?

Mary Are we love? Oh that's nice.

Debra Nice? Auntie, it's a nightmare.

Mary It's ironic isn't it, us being down here again.

Debra What do you mean again?

Mary You, me and Charlie.

Debra *(putting her arm around Mary)* Auntie… Charlie's dead..

Mary Oh what am I saying, of course he is..

Debra So, have you got any ideas as to how we can get out of this cellar?

Mary It doesn't have a handle on the inside.

Debra I know that Auntie..

Mary I took it off you see.

Debra I wish you hadn't.

Mary Poor Charlie.

Debra Yes, poor Charlie… but isn't there any other way out of here?

Mary He wanted to get out too you see.

Debra I know Auntie, you told me..he loved you.

Mary I asked him to take a look at the tank, he was good with things like that..folk were always asking him to fix things.

Debra What tank?

Mary Jenny had gone to stay with her mother for a while. I used to go round to help look after Charlie for her. *(Mary moves towards the sleeping Jean.)* She was so stupid, so trusting, she had no idea about Charlie and me.

Debra What do you mean?

Mary He felt guilty. He told me he couldn't leave her. Can you imagine that? I mean look at her, she never had the looks or the figure I had. All she had was that rotten little kid that she dangled in front of him.

Debra *(backs away nervously)* So what happened Auntie?

Mary It wasn't his fault. He was weak, she was too strong for him and it was up to me to protect him, to keep him away from her.

Debra Did you shut the door to the cellar Auntie?

Mary It was the only way you see. I couldn't let her have him could I? I had to keep him safe. So I took the door handle off.

Debra You left him down there… for how long Auntie, for how long?

Mary I couldn't listen to his screams. I used to sit in the garden for hours, he took such a long time to stop screaming.

Debra How could you do that? How could you just leave him down there to die.

Mary I only ever wanted us to be together, you understand that don't you?

Debra Poor Jenny.

Mary Oh yes well that was the final irony. You see, when Jenny came back, no-one could tell her where Charlie was. She used to sit and wait by the window hoping to catch sight of him coming up the road and all the time he was dying underneath her feet. It was Christmas Eve when they finally found the body. Of course nobody believed Jenny was innocent. Everybody had known that Charlie and me were an item, and the jury just assumed that it was her jealousy that had driven her to it. It was easy.

Debra All this time you've let her suffer for what you have done.

Mary She deserved it I tell you.

Debra Nobody deserves what you did Aunt, nobody.

Mary It doesn't matter now anyway, no-one will ever know.

Debra I'll know. I can't just brush this under the carpet. You killed a man Auntie and then let his poor wife serve twenty-four years in prison, not to mention giving up her child, how could you do that?

Mary Because she deserved it..all of it. Charlie loved me, really loved me and yet she couldn't let him go, he told her about us and she wouldn't let him go.

(Jean suddenly opens her eyes.)

Jean He never told me.

Mary *(turns on Jean, her eyes full of hatred)* That's not true.

Jean *(standing)* It is true. He never told me about you, or being unhappy.. I never knew

Mary He was miserable with you.

Jean I never knew.

Mary All your stupid supper parties and your badminton club do's, he hated it, every minute of it. He couldn't wait to get away from you, he couldn't wait to get into my bed at night, to be with a woman who made him feel like a man, not just some suburban status symbol.

Jean Stop it.

Mary Why, why couldn't you let him go.?

Jean He never asked me.

Mary Liar.

Jean It's the truth.

Mary Liar, liar, liar. *(Puts her hands over her ears and screams this line over and over again.)*

Jean *(crying, repeats her line too)* I didn't know. I didn't know.

Debra For god's sake stop it, please stop it.

(Debra pulls then apart, Mary turns away, rocking herself and repeating the line, more softly.)

Jean I would have let him go if that would have saved him would have let him go.

Debra Did you know that she killed him?

Jean He was there all that time and I didn't know..I could have saved him, it's my fault, I could have saved him.

Debra None of this is your fault. You've been wronged Mrs Ham... Jenny, terribly wronged, my aunt is completely insane, and as soon as we get out of here we are going straight to the police.

Mary *(suddenly laughs wildly)* Listen to you, 'as soon as we get out of here we are going straight to the police'. *(Mary turns on them)* How? How are you going to get out... nobody knows you are here do they?

Debra Sooner or later someone will find us.

Mary But will it be soon... or just too late.

Jean I think I'm going to have to sit down.

Debra *(rushes over to Jean and helps her into the deckchair)* Are you OK?

Jean   Just a bit breathless. I'll be all right in a minute.

Debra *(turns towards Mary)* You see what you have done..

Mary   You think I care.

Debra You're a monster... and to think that for all these years I thought you were some sweet, innocent old auntie and all the time you are some sort of sadistic nutcase who sent an innocent woman to prison for a murder you committed.

Mary   Oh as if it makes any difference to you Miss Hoity Toity Chambers. Don't kid yourself that you cared about me. You only came here because your family brought you. As soon as you got yourself hitched to that no hoper husband of yours you forgot all about me.

Debra That's not true.

Mary   Isn't it? Then tell me, when was the last time you came to see me for a chat or offered to help out with the shopping or took me out for a walk? Tell me when that was..

Debra I have a life you know, just because I didn't visit as much as I should have doesn't mean to say that I didn't care

Mary   You only came here today because I hadn't sent you a birthday card didn't you?

Debra I was concerned, though god knows why.

Mary   You were concerned? More like you missed the ten pound note that I always put in.

Debra Oh don't be ridiculous.

Mary   It was the only way to get you here..and it worked.

Debra What, so you're telling me you forgot my birthday intentionally? All you had to do was pick up the phone and I would have come straight-away.

Mary   I wanted you to find me, and I knew if you turned up she's be hanging about, she always had her nose pressed to the window, she wouldn't be able to resist coming over. It was all a bit too easy.

Debra What are you saying?

Jean   She got us here deliberately.

Mary   Oh well done, have a sugar lump both of you..I've run out of gold stars.

Debra But why? Why did you want us both here? Did you want to confess..is that was this is all about, because if you think that for one minute I am going to throw my arms around you and say I forgive you, you can think again you disgust me.

Mary Oh dear..did you hear that Jenny..I disgust her. Charlie would have been so upset to have heard her say that.

Debra Who gives a stuff about what Charlie would have thought. I couldn't give a damn. I just want to get out of here, it's getting too claustrophobic. *(Debra starts to panic, she attempts to get past Mary who just laughs in her face. Escapes and runs towards door, breathing heavily. Mary grabs her arm and swings her round. Debra screams and pulls away, Mary laughs. Debra reaches door and frantically begins to hammer her fists onto it.)* Help, somebody help me. Can anyone hear me? Help, Help.

Mary She's beginning to panic.. can you feel it? This must have been how Charlie felt. First the confidence, the hope and then the panic, the perhaps no-one will ever come feeling.

Jean My chest is getting tighter. I can't get my breath.

Mary *(sarcastically)* Oh dear, you too? Whatever shall we do?

(Lights down to denote the passing of time. Lights up. Debra is sitting on bottom step, head in hands. Jean dead in deckchair. Mary sitting down playing with sugar in sugar bowl.)

Debra *(raising her head, she seems nervous, edgy)* What time is it?

Mary Does it really matter?

Debra How long have we been down here?

Mary Three days.

Debra Oh my god. I need a drink.

Mary She'll start to smell soon.

Debra I still can't believe it, poor woman, her heart must have just given up on her.

Mary I'm glad she's dead.

Debra *(in tears)* Why, why are you glad? She'd done nothing to you. She was just some poor old lady that had spent most of her life suffering for what you had done. Look at her, she didn't deserve this, any of this. She should have been allowed to enjoy what life she had left..but you've taken that too haven't you. Poor Jean.

Mary She stood in my way. You both stood in my way.

Debra So that's justification is it. 'She stood in my way'. Who the hell do you think you are that you can destroy people, simply because you, *you* can't have what you want. Have you ever considered that perhaps Charlie didn't actually want you, that he loved Jenny and the reason he hadn't told her about you was because he never had any intention of leaving her... because you were nothing more than a bit of fun.

Mary Well you would say that wouldn't you, because if it hadn't been for you none of this would have happened.

Debra Me? What on earth did I do? I didn't even know her or your bloody Charlie.

Mary Oh but you did.

Debra *(gets up and moves towards Mary. Debra's hair is messy and her face has dirt on it)* How?

Mary If she hadn't had you..he would have left.

Debra I don't understand.

Mary *(gets up and faces Debra)* It was *you*, you were the kid, the reason Charlie wouldn't leave her.

Debra Me... but that's rubbish. I had a dad, don't you remember.

Mary Charlie was my cousin, when they put her away they handed you over to my brother and his wife.

Debra No, this is a lie. This is just your way of twisting the knife to make me suffer for your pain.

Mary Seen any baby photos have you? Got any piccies of you and your folks before your second birthday.

Debra I would have known, they would have told me.

Mary Told you what? That your mother was a murderer. That she had let your dear old dad die in the cellar of your home while you played with your dollies upstairs... No, they wanted to protect you, keep you in the dark. We weren't even allowed to visit Charlie's grave because of *you*.

Debra I don't believe you. I don't believe you..

Mary Shame she died before I could tell her you were her daughter. I could have played Cilla.

Mary *(Mary starts to sing loudly)* Surprise, surprise.

Debra Shut up.

Mary The moment hits you right between the eyes.

Debra Shut up. *I said shut up, shut up, shut up.*

(Debra puts her hands around Mary's throat and starts to strangle her. Mary pulls knife from her pocket and stabs Debra. As Debra falls to her knees, a mobile phone begins to ring from the corner of the stage. Mary walks over to where it is hidden and

retrieves it, placing it in front of Debra.)

Mary Oh would you look at that, you had a way out after all. I'd forgotten about my phone. *(Debra reaches for it and Mary kicks it away.)* Oh dear, I don't think you're going to get to it, now isn't that just the most annoying thing. *(Debra collapses. Mary smiles, she carefully begins to tidy the bodies as she delivers her speech.)* Not long now Charlie. I knew you wouldn't want to leave them behind. I've brought them to you Charlie..so we can be together. Nothing stands in between us now love... we will all be together again. No-one can keep us apart any longer. *(Produces a lipstick from her pocket and proceeds to put some on, smearing it across her face. Suddenly there is a loud banging on the door.)*

Dave Miss Perkins... it's me, Dave the milkman. I was a bit worried when you didn't answer yesterday so I came back to check you were okay. The police are here too, they let me in. *(Coming down the steps)* Ah there you are Miss Perkins... Miss Perkins? Sergeant, I think you better come down here.

Mary *(screams wretchedly) No. (Drops to her knees as lights go down.)*

End

www.ingramcontent.com/pod-product-compliance
Lightning Source LLC
Chambersburg PA
CBHW060608030426
42337CB00019B/3661